W9-ALL-909

WORLD BOOK'S
LIBRARY OF NATURAL DISASTERS

WILDFIRES

WORLD
BOOK

a Scott Fetzer company
Chicago
www.worldbookonline.com

World Book, Inc.
233 N. Michigan Avenue
Chicago, IL 60601
U.S.A.

For information about other World Book publications, visit our Web site at **http://www.worldbookonline.com** or call **1-800-WORLDBK (967-5325).**

For information about sales to schools and libraries, call **1-800-975-3250 (United States)**; **1-800-837-5365 (Canada).**

2008 revised printing

Library of Congress Cataloging-in-Publication Data

Wildfires.
    p. cm. -- (World Book's library of natural disasters)
    Summary: "A discussion of a major type of natural disaster, including descriptions of some of the most destructive; explanations of these phenomena, what causes them, and where they occur; and information about how to prepare for and survive these forces of nature. Features include an activity, glossary, list of resources, and index"--Provided by publisher.
    Includes bibliographical references and index.
    ISBN 978-0-7166-9816-6
    1. Wildfires--Juvenile literature. I. World Book, Inc.
SD421.23.W55 2007
363.37'9--dc22
             2007008820

World Book's Library of Natural Disasters
Set ISBN: 978-0-7166-9801-2

Printed in China
2 3 4 5 6 12 11 10 09 08

Editor in Chief: Paul A. Kobasa

Supplementary Publications
    Associate Director: Scott Thomas
    Managing Editor: Barbara A. Mayes

Editors: Jeff De La Rosa, Nicholas Kilzer, Christine Sullivan, Kristina A. Vaicikonis, Marty Zwikel

Researchers: Cheryl Graham, Jacqueline Jasek

Manager, Editorial Operations
    (Rights & Permissions): Loranne K. Shields

Graphics and Design
    Associate Director: Sandra M. Dyrlund
    Associate Manager, Design: Brenda B. Tropinski
    Associate Manager, Photography: Tom Evans
    Designer: Matt Carrington

Product development: Arcturus Publishing Limited
Writer: Anne Rooney
Editor: Nicola Barber, Alex Woolf
Designer: Talking Design
Illustrator: Stefan Chabluk

Acknowledgments:

Alaska Fire Service: cover/ title page (John McColgan).

Corbis: 4 (Frans Lanting), 6 (AIM Patrice/ Corbis Sygma), 7 (Olivier Coret/ In Visu), 9 (Bettmann), 13 (Earl & Nazima Kowall), 14, 27, 29, 39, 42 (Raymond Gehman), 16 (Maggie Hallahan), 17 (Mark Avery/ Orange County Register), 21 (Michael Goulding/ Orange County Register), 23 (Steve Kaufman), 24 (Rick Doyle), 25 (Hulton-Deutsch Collection), 28 (Galen Rowell), 31 (Penny Tweedie), 32, 36 (Reuters), 34 (James L. Amos), 35 (Steve Terrill), 38 (Bruce Chambers/ Orange County Register), 43 (K.J. Historical).

Knowledge Resource Centre, Department of Primary Industries, Victoria: 22.

Minnesota Historical Society: 18, 19.

NASA: 33 (Jacques Descloitres/ MODIS Land Rapid Response Team at NASA GSFC, 37 (U.S. Forest Service).

Science Photo Library: 5 (W.K. Fletcher), 15, 30, 40, 41 (Kari Greer), 20 (NASA).

Shutterstock: 10 (Anna Galejeva).

TABLE OF CONTENTS

Glossary There is a glossary of terms on pages 45-46. Terms defined in the glossary are in type **that looks like this** on their first appearance on any spread (two facing pages).

Additional resources Books for further reading and recommended Web sites are listed on page 47. Because of the nature of the Internet, some Web site addresses may have changed since publication. The publisher has no responsibility for any such changes or for the content of cited sources.

WHAT IS A WILDFIRE?

Flames leap high into the air as a wildfire rages in Big Sur, California.

A wildfire is a fire that rages out of control through forest or **brush.** It may destroy everything in its path and can produce terrifying, whirling storms of fire. Wildfires usually begin in unpopulated areas, but they can approach human settlements and urban areas, where they become very dangerous to people. Every year in the United States, some 135,000 wildfires burn across nearly 4 million acres (1.6 million hectares). Worldwide, wildfires annually burn across about 30 million acres (12 million hectares) of land.

Natural and human causes

Human beings cause most wildfires, either by accident or on purpose. Many other wildfires are caused by lightning strikes. Wildfires have occurred naturally for as long as there have been forests.

Where wildfires occur

Wildfires typically take place as the result of certain conditions, particularly **drought,** which causes **vegetation** to dry out. Such fires are common in the Australian **bush;** in California and the southern plains of the United States; the forests of Southeast Asia, China, Russia, and southern Europe; and the grasslands and forests of Africa and South America.

Essential to the planet

Wildfires cause tremendous destruction, but they are also vital to the growth cycles of forests. A healthy forest renews itself when fire clears away old, dead wood, making space for new growth to flourish. Wildfires provide a natural way for this process to occur. In many parts of the world, park authorities—including the United States National Park Service—allow some wildfires that do not endanger people or property to burn, letting nature take its course.

HOW BIG IS THE PROBLEM?

Some wildfires burn over huge areas of land. In 1881, a wildfire in Michigan burned 1 million acres (400,000 hectares) of virgin white pine forest. About 50,000 fires occur each year in regions along the Mediterranean Sea. Wildfires also result in a loss of life. Each year, many firefighters are killed battling such fires.

Seed cones from a *Banksia* tree show the effects of a fire. The heat from the fire opens the seed capsules to release the seeds. *Banksia* is a common shrub in the Australian bush.

CAUSES OF WILDFIRES

A tiny spark can start a fire that may destroy millions of acres of forest. Once a fire starts, it can, under the right conditions, rapidly swell into a wildfire. Many fires begin as a result of human accident. A cigarette dropped by a hiker or a campfire left smoldering by a park visitor can cause fires that may have terrible consequences. Sparks from vehicle exhausts or people burning trash are also common accidental causes of fires. Farmers and building developers often use fires to remove tree and other plant growth from cleared forestland. These fires can easily get out of control.

Arson

Some people intentionally start fires to cause damage, a crime known as **arson.** Occasionally, individuals start fires just to see them burn. In other cases, people may commit arson to make an insurance claim on a

Arson was the probable cause of a wildfire in Castellet, France, that spread across 2,000 acres (800 hectares) in 2001.

building. In Brazil, Indonesia, and other tropical areas, landowners set fires to clear the rain forests for farming and herding.

Natural causes

Fires may start naturally in several ways. Lightning is one of the most common causes. In the southern U.S. state of Florida, lightning causes 19 percent of all wildfires. When **combustible** wood reaches a high enough temperature, it can ignite on its own without an outside trigger. This type of burning, called **spontaneous combustion,** commonly causes fires in dry **vegetation.** In some places, **eruptions** from **volcanoes** can start wildfires. Red-hot, flowing rock called lava or the scorching winds that surge from a volcano can easily set fire to vegetation.

A LAVA FIRE

On May 18, 2002, a wildfire raged on Kilauea, Hawaii, that was caused by a lava flow. The fire scorched more than 4,000 acres (1,619 hectares) of rain forest, including rare plants found nowhere else in the world. Four helicopters and 40 firefighters eventually doused the flames by dropping water from above and cutting down trees to create a **firebreak.**

Lava from a 2002 eruption of Mount Etna, a volcano on the Italian island of Sicily, causes a wildfire as the molten rock ignites trees in its path.

THE GREAT PESHTIGO FIRE

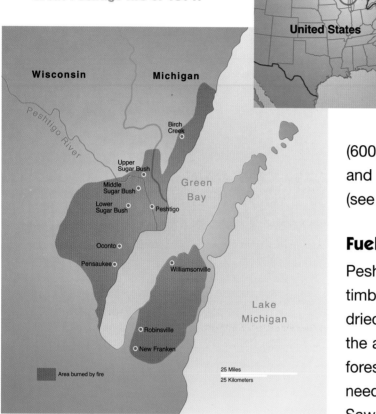

The area burned by the Great Peshtigo fire of 1871.

United States

Wisconsin   Michigan

Peshtigo River

Birch Creek

Upper Sugar Bush

Middle Sugar Bush

Lower Sugar Bush   Peshtigo

Green Bay

Oconto

Pensaukee

Williamsonville

Lake Michigan

Robinsville

New Franken

Area burned by fire

25 Miles
25 Kilometers

The deadliest wildfire in U.S. history occurred on Oct. 8, 1871, near the town of Peshtigo, in northeastern Wisconsin. The fire killed about 1,200 people—the single largest death toll from fire in U.S. history. The wildfire burned across 1.5 million acres (600,000 hectares) of pine forest in Wisconsin and Michigan. In Peshtigo itself, the **fire storm** (see page 24) left only one building standing.

Fuel everywhere

Peshtigo was a small town surrounded by vast timberland. In 1871, widespread **drought** had dried out the ponds, creeks, and swamps in the area. The drought had also dried the forest, causing evergreen trees to shed their needles and hardwoods to drop their leaves. Sawmills contributed to the debris on the forest floor. It was common lumbering practice at the time to leave part of each tree behind, surrounded by sawdust and piles of waste called slash. By autumn, the region had become a tinderbox.

Many small fires become one big fire

Historians don't know for sure how or where the Peshtigo fire started. Many believe that strong winds fanned countless small fires that had been started by people to clear the forest. In the evening of October 8, walls of flame

FIRES FROM SPACE?

Some scientists have suggested that the Peshtigo fire, as well as the Great Chicago fire—which took place on the same night—might have been caused by a meteor shower. Such showers are common in the upper Midwest in autumn. Occasionally, chunks of rock or metal fall from space and reach the ground before burning up completely. These **meteorites** do sometimes start fires.

roared across the land, driven by winds blowing at speeds of 90 to 100 miles (145 to 160 kilometers) per hour. When the fire reached the settlement of Peshtigo, it tore through the wooden buildings.

A contemporary engraving depicts the confusion and panic triggered in people and animals by the great fire in Peshtigo, Wisconsin, on Oct. 8, 1871.

Peshtigo's destruction

Overnight, the raging fire consumed the town of Peshtigo as well as other towns and farms. So many people died that after the fire, more than 400 bodies had to be buried in a mass grave. Many people survived only by throwing themselves into the Peshtigo River or any other body of water they could find and submerging themselves to escape the heat. One report stated sadly: "Whole neighborhoods hav[e] been swept away without any warning, or leaving any trace, or record to tell the tale. It has been a difficult task to collect the number and names of families who have wholly or in part perished."

THE CHEMISTRY OF FIRE

Fires need three things to start and continue burning: fuel; a source of heat to ignite the fuel; and **oxygen** to keep the fire burning. Firefighters put out fires by eliminating at least one of these three essential elements.

Fuel

Any **flammable** material can serve as fuel. Wildfires are usually fueled by wood and other dry **vegetation.** When a wildfire reaches a settlement, buildings—and the gas, oil, and coal used by people—also fuel the fire. The fuels that feed a wildfire are often divided into three types:

The surface fuels that feed a forest-type fire generally consist of leaves, twigs, fallen branches, and trees less than 6 feet (1.8 meters) in height.

- **Ground fuels** lie beneath Earth's surface. They include buried pieces of wood, decayed plant matter and tree roots, and dried **peat.**
- **Surface fuels** lie on the ground. They include dried grasses and other types of low-growing vegetation; fallen leaves, twigs, and branches; and low-growing shrubs and trees measuring less than 6 feet (1.8 meters) tall.
- **Aerial fuels** consist of any material located more than 6 feet above the ground. Such fuels include the leaves and branches of trees and any moss or vines growing on them.

Oxygen

Oxygen is a gas that makes up about 21 percent of the air. As a fire burns, oxygen in the air combines with carbon and hydrogen in the fuel, producing carbon dioxide (CO_2), carbon monoxide (CO), and water (H_2O). These chemical reactions also produce heat, which is why a fire's flames feel hot. Winds fan the flames of a fire because they bring more oxygen to keep the fire burning. The fire leaves behind **ash** and sometimes **charcoal.**

How heat travels

Heat from wildfires travels mostly by the process of **convection.** Hot air from the fire rises and cooler air takes its place, heating up in turn. This process creates a flow of rising warm air and falling cold air, called a **convection current.**

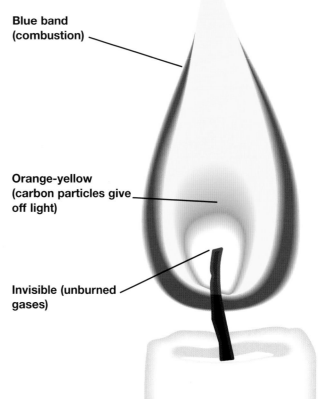

Blue band (combustion)

Orange-yellow (carbon particles give off light)

Invisible (unburned gases)

COLORFUL FLAMES

The colors of a flame depend on the material being burned and the temperature of the fire. On a wax candle, the blue band around the flame is the burning part of a fire, where **combustion** occurs. It is the hottest part of the flame. The orange-yellow part consists of tiny, unburned particles of carbon. The particles are so hot that they glow, giving off light. The center of the flame is invisible and consists of unburned gases. Flames coming from other materials have different proportions of these colors. A wood fire, for example, looks mostly bright orange because wood burns a lot more carbon, and it burns at lower temperatures than does a candle.

THE GREAT BLACK DRAGON FIRE

In May 1987, the Great Black Dragon fire, perhaps the biggest wildfire in history, raged across parts of China and Russia (then part of the Union of Soviet Socialist Republics, or the Soviet Union). It swept through the forests of Manchuria in China and of Siberia in Russia, scorching millions of acres. Chinese authorities reported more than 200 dead, about as many injured, and 56,000 homeless in Manchuria alone. However, these figures are probably lower than the actual number of casualties. Russian authorities never released figures for the people affected in Siberia.

A secret land

In the 1980's, the Greater Hinggan Forest was the world's largest evergreen forest. It measured some 500 miles (800 kilometers) long and 300 miles (480 kilometers) wide. The Heilongjiang, or Black Dragon River (called the Amur in Russia), runs through the forest and forms the border between China and Russia. In 1987, both China and the Soviet

The Great Black Dragon fire burned across more than 3 million acres (1.2 million hectares) of forest in China in 1987. Although the Soviet Union never disclosed the full extent of the fire in Siberia, an estimated 9 to 15 million acres (3.6 to 6 million hectares) burned.

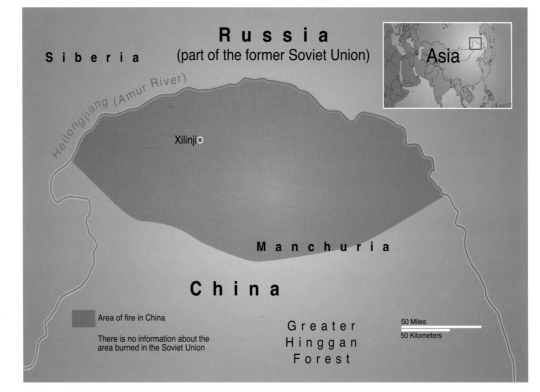

Russia
(part of the former Soviet Union)

Siberia

Heilongjiang (Amur River)

Xilinji

Asia

Manchuria

China

Area of fire in China

There is no information about the area burned in the Soviet Union

Greater Hinggan Forest

50 Miles

50 Kilometers

Union kept this region largely closed to foreign visitors. As a result, the countries released very little information about the fire to the outside world.

Burning for a month

The Great Black Dragon fire raged out of control for more than a month in the spring of 1987. It was finally extinguished by rain. Most of the firefighters who battled the blaze had little experience. In China, the army and the local inhabitants tried to beat back the flames. On both sides of the river, firefighters had only the most basic equipment and little knowledge of techniques for fighting forest fires. In addition, the Russian and Chinese firefighting teams did not communicate and only battled the fires on their own side of the river.

Terrible destruction

China lost more than 3 million acres (1.2 million hectares) of forest in the 1987 blaze, nearly one-fourth of the country's timber reserve. Russia may have lost from 9 to 15 million acres (3.6 to 6 million hectares), though Russian authorities did not release any figures. The combined forest ranked as the largest stand of trees in the world and contained possibly one-tenth of the world's **conifers.**

The fire projected a wall of flame that at times moved at speeds as high as 60 miles (100 kilometers) per hour. The flames completely destroyed towns, including Xilinji, in Manchuria. Fortunately, the 18,000 inhabitants had been evacuated.

AN UNFORTUNATE ACCIDENT

The Great Black Dragon fire began as several small fires in different places, which joined to create one big fire. One section was started accidentally by 18-year-old Wang Yufeng. Wang was in the forest cutting back **brush** to reduce the risk of fire and spilled gasoline that he was using to power his cutting device. Wang was later imprisoned for his accident.

A fire official displays an explosive used by his department to fight the wildfire that burned the town of Xilinji, China.

HOW FIRES SPREAD AND RESTART

A truck emerges from a smoke cloud created by one of the fires that burned in Yellowstone National Park, Wyoming, in 1988.

Wildfires can spread extremely quickly across the ground or through treetops, depending on the surface and air conditions. Wildfires occur most often in the summer and fall, when hot weather and lack of rain have dried out **vegetation** and there are strong winds to fan the flames.

Types of fire

Researchers often classify fires as one of three different types:

- A **ground fire** burns in the ground-fuel layer, and so it spreads underground. It produces no flames, but smoke seeps out of the ground.
- A **surface fire** burns surface fuels, moving through grass, **brush,** and low trees. When these materials form an unbroken layer on the ground, a surface fire can spread easily.
- A **crown fire** burns the *crowns* (upper branches and leaves) of trees. It happens when a surface fire finds a "ladder," a dry tree or other tall fuel that can carry the fire upward. Steep slopes or strong winds can allow crown fires to grow and quickly move uphill (see pages 20–21).

Spreading fires

Some fires creep along the ground and typically spread slowly and so are easily contained. Others fires spread by a more dangerous process called **spotting.** Burning **embers** carried on the wind start a new fire some distance from the original. Spotting allows fires to spread rapidly over a large area. New fires start and combine, joining up with the original fire. Spotting fires are sometimes called "jumping fires" because they can jump across places where there is no fuel, including rivers and roads.

Restarting

If firefighters put out a fire, or if a fire goes out because of rain or falling temperatures, it can still reignite. Some fires die down at night and then spring up again in the morning when ground temperatures rise. Fires may also travel underground, as ground fires, and then reemerge above ground where they ignite **surface fuels** far from the original fire.

THE YELLOWSTONE FIRES

The largest series of fires in the northern Rockies in 78 years burned through parts of Yellowstone National Park, which is primarily in Wyoming, in 1988. During the peak days in early September, the area scorched by the fires increased by more than 615,000 acres (249,000 hectares). Because of lightning and human actions, fires started and restarted until more than 988,000 acres (400,000 hectares)—nearly half of the park—burned. About 9,500 firefighters failed to stop the flames. In September, snow finally extinguished the fires.

Firefighters run to extinguish a spotting fire during a wildfire in Colorado.

THE CEDAR FIRE

A firefighting helicopter drops chemicals to try to put out a blaze during the Cedar fire of 2003.

The Cedar fire, the largest documented wildfire in California, raged through Cleveland National Forest in the fall of 2003, burning 280,000 acres (113,000 hectares). The Cedar fire was 1 of at least 13 fires that were burning in California at the time. The fires destroyed a combined area of 600,000 acres (240,000 hectares) of forest.

How a small fire grew

On October 25, a hunter who had become lost lit a signal fire south of Ramona, in San Diego County, hoping to alert searchers to his whereabouts. Because of dry conditions, the fire he set spread quickly, and in just over 10 hours it burned over 80,000 acres (32,375 hectares) of forest. Like the other fires burning in the area, the Cedar fire was fanned by the Santa Ana winds, which bring hot, dry air from the desert to the east. These winds spread the fire rapidly and contributed to extremely dangerous features, including **fire whirls**—fiery tornadolike columns of swirling wind with superheated centers.

Fighting the flames

Three days after it started, the Cedar fire destroyed the community of Cuyamaca, 40 miles (64 kilometers) east of San Diego. The flames then threatened the town of Julian in San Diego County. Nearly 1,500 firefighters battled the fire with water and other **fire retardants** from above. Helicopters scooped up water to drop onto the flames, and planes sprayed chemicals over the area. About 125 fire trucks protected most of Julian. Nevertheless, the fire destroyed 2,232 houses and left 14 people dead.

THE MIRAMICHI FIRE

The largest recorded fire in eastern North America began on Oct. 6, 1825, in New Brunswick, Canada. The fire began in an area that was being extensively **logged.** At the time, fires purposely were kept burning day and night both inside and outside buildings because, before matches were invented, it was difficult to start a fire. People still do not know the cause of the Miramichi fire. But most reports estimated that from 2.5 to 5 million acres (1 to 2 million hectares) of forest burned— about one-fifth the area of New Brunswick. The fire also spread into northern Maine. About 150 people died in the blaze, and it wiped out entire settlements. However, the homeless settlers received clothing, money, and supplies from other areas of Canada, the United Kingdom, and the United States.

A house near Julian in San Diego County is engulfed in flames during the Cedar fire.

LOGGING FIRES

Wildfires commonly occur in areas where people cut timber. Piles of drying logs, unwanted **brush** and smaller branches, sawed timber, and vast amounts of sawdust all provide ample fuel for a fire. **Logging** equipment and vehicles often produce sparks, and loggers often start fires to clear undergrowth. As a result, logging fires have been a hazard for as long as people have been clearing the land of trees.

The Cloquet fire

From Oct. 13 through 15, 1918, a massive fire destroyed 1.2 million acres (0.5 million hectares) of forest and 38 towns and villages in northern Minnesota and Wisconsin. The fire started when sparks from a steam-powered train engine ignited parched grass and piles of cut timber that had been left beside railway lines. Fanned by strong fall winds, the fire raged through the forest and destroyed the village of Moose Lake. The city of Cloquet burned to the ground, with only a few sawmills left standing. Although many of the inhabitants of Moose Lake and Cloquet escaped, the Cloquet fire left at least 1,000 people dead, including 453 victims in Cloquet.

Automobiles lie abandoned in Moose Lake after the Cloquet forest fire in 1918.

A photograph of Hinckley, Minnesota, taken the morning after the fire of 1894 reveals the near-total devastation.

The Hinckley fire

A fire ravaged Hinckley, Minnesota, on Sept. 1, 1894, when two small fires combined and then escalated into a raging **fire storm** (see pages 24–25). In just four hours, the fire destroyed 6 towns and about 160,000 acres (65,000 hectares) of forest. A long **drought** had left the region unusually dry, and loggers had *overcut* the area (cut more trees than can be regrown). Dry scrub and debris left by the loggers burned rapidly. When the fire reached the stores of logged wood near settlements and mills, the flames quickly ignited buildings and soon the whole town was on fire.

Scorching air rose high above the ground, sucking up enough **oxygen** at ground level to make many people suffocate. The Hinckley fire killed 418 people. *The New York Times* reported tangles of charred bodies awaiting burial piled up like "so many dried sticks." Some people escaped by climbing aboard passing trains on a railroad line constructed to transport lumber out of the heavily forested region.

HIDING FROM THE FIRE

About 300 people survived the Hinckley fire by crouching low in 18 inches (46 centimeters) of mud in Skunk Lake. Another 100 people escaped the fire by climbing down into the town's gravel pit. Inhabitants of Moose Lake ran for the nearby icy Kettle River. One survivor at Hinckley, Mollie McNeill, described how she hid in mud at Skunk Lake: "I remained in the swamp all night. I put my face in the mud to cool it, and some one plastered mud all over my hair." Other survivors told of wolves and bears that had been driven to the water but were too afraid of the fire to attack the people there.

WHAT CONDITIONS AFFECT FIRES?

Strong winds drive smoke ahead of wildfires burning out of control in California's San Bernadino Mountains, in October 2003, in an image captured from the International Space Station.

Wildfires typically develop when smaller fires race out of control. Smaller fires swell and spread depending on the conditions around them. The slope of the ground, the direction of the wind, and other aspects of the weather all help to determine which fires become catastrophic and which fires fizzle out.

The lay of the land

A land region's form and shape, or its **topography,** can affect a fire's behavior. If a fire reaches an upward slope, it can burn fiercely and race uphill. As hot air from the fire rises, it dries out **vegetation** on the land above, preparing the fuel to burn more easily. Sparks may rise upward and set fire to vegetation farther up the slope. In contrast, a downward slope slows the progress of a fire.

Weather conditions

Dry weather, which dries out fuel, can contribute to the spread of fire. Fire is less likely to take hold in humid conditions. Rain, snow, and hail can also slow or stop a fire.

Wind drives the growth of a fire in two ways. It blows the hot air, flames, and sparks toward new fuel, drying and heating the fuel and sometimes starting new fires. Wind also brings **oxygen** to the fire, accelerating the burning. In addition, strong winds can have a great effect on the speed at which a fire spreads.

ANATOMY OF A FIRE

A wildfire usually appears oval in shape and grows outward at the edges. The combination of wind and topography typically causes the fire to advance more quickly in one direction, stretching the oval. The **head** of the fire is the part that advances fastest. It often travels in the direction of the wind or uphill. The flanks, or sides, of the fire move outward more slowly. The tail end of the fire moves at the slowest speed because it has to move against the wind or downhill. The wind and slope carry the tail into the already burned area at the center of the fire.

Fog and rain dampen fires that had raged out of control in Southern California in 2003. Precipitation often douses wildfires that could not be brought under control by firefighters.

AUSTRALIAN BUSHFIRES

A building in West Healesville, Victoria, is consumed by flames during the devastating wildfire that raged across the state on Jan. 13, 1939.

Many parts of Australia have hot, dry climates and vast expanses of forest and **bush**. In times of **drought,** humidity can drop to as low as 20 percent, compared with an average humidity of from 40 to 70 percent. In addition, the water level in **vegetation** can drop to less than one-half of its normal level.

Wildfires commonly occur in the Australian bush and can very quickly burn out of control. Most fires occur when the weather is driest. In the north, the dry season runs from May to October. In the south, the dry season is from December to February.

Blackened soil surrounds eucalyptus trees after a fire in the Black Mountain Reserve in Australia. Trees often bear the scars of wildfires for decades after the event.

The Black Friday fire

On Jan. 13, 1939, Australia experienced the worst wildfire in its history. The fire burned nearly 5 million acres (2 million hectares) in the state of Victoria. The Black Friday fire completely destroyed several towns and killed 71 people. The Royal Commission set up to investigate the fire reported that "it appeared the whole State was alight."

In the days leading up to the fire, temperatures in Melbourne, the capital of Victoria, were among the highest ever recorded. On the day of the fire, the temperature in Melbourne climbed to 114.1 °F (45.6 °C), the hottest day on record. Strong northerly winds drove several small fires together, which formed a single massive fire front. The fires raged until January 15, when rain finally doused the flames.

Long after the fire, local water sources remained contaminated by **ash** and debris. Ash from the fire fell as far away as New Zealand. Because of a drought that preceded the fire and the scope and intensity of the blaze, the soil took decades to recover, and large areas of animal habitat were lost. There are trees still standing after nearly 70 years that show signs of having been scorched by the Black Friday fire of 1939.

FLAMMABLE PLANTS

Some plants burn so well that their presence contributes to the spread of wildfires. The eucalyptus genus of trees and shrubs contains a high amount of an oil that is highly **flammable.** Eucalyptus regrows quickly after a fire, taking over land that fire has cleared of other vegetation. As a result, the oil gives eucalyptus an advantage over other plants. Eucalyptus grows across Australia, and its success has been helped by the arrival of human beings, about 50,000 years ago, who started fires to clear land. However, the prevalence of eucalyptus now encourages fires unwanted by human residents.

A fire that swells into a raging inferno can create its own drafts. As a result, the fire fans its own flames in a phenomenon known as a **fire storm.** Severe fires may also produce **fire whirls,** in which tornadolike swirls of scorching winds and flames devour everything in their path.

Convection columns

As hot air rises, it leaves a space that is filled by cold air coming in from either above or around the edges of the rising **convection column.** In a fire, a convection column appears as a dense tower of smoke because the rising hot air carries burning **embers** and particles of soot. However, a convection column cannot form over land with strong surface winds. Convection columns rise to heights of from 25,000 to 50,000 feet (7,600 to 15,000 meters).

Rising hot air carrying embers and soot from a wildfire in California produces a convection column, a dense tower of smoke.

Fire storms

Fire storms are massive fires with intense heat. A fire storm can occur when the wind drops or when a fire meets an area of dense fuel. Air

rising up the convection column strengthens into a strong **updraft,** causing heat to build up rapidly. Showers of embers from the convection column can set fire to surrounding trees or buildings. Fire storms may occur during wildfires, but they can also develop in bombed urban areas. During World War II (1939-1945), U.S. and British military staff studied the Peshtigo fire storm of 1871 to learn how to create fire storms during firebombing attacks on such cities as Dresden, Germany, and Tokyo, Japan.

Fire whirls

A tornadolike whirl of fiery wind can develop from warm updrafts in a convection column. Under the right conditions of wind and air temperature, the convection column becomes a **vortex**—a spinning column of hot air and gases. A fire whirl sucks up flames and debris as it moves over the land.

Fire whirls range from about 1 foot (0.3 meter) to 500 feet (150 meters) in diameter. Most fire whirls measure no higher than about 150 feet (46 meters), but some reach heights of several hundred feet.

Firebombs dropped on the German city of Dresden during World War II caused massive fire storms that left much of the city in ruins and thousands of residents dead.

THE FIRE STORM OF THE HINCKLEY FIRE

The Hinckley fire of 1894 (see pages 18–19) started on a hot day, but the arrival of cold air from the west transformed the fire into a fire storm. The cold air pressed down on the fire, holding the heat, smoke, and burning gases close to the ground and intensifying the heat. As the heat of the flames reached the cold air above, the air rushed down to feed the fire, creating a swirl of flames that grew larger and larger, swelling into a massive fire storm.

THE BIG BURN OF 1910

In the summer of 1910, fire roared through the forests of Idaho and Montana, destroying 3 million acres (1.2 million hectares) of forest in two days. In terms of area, the fire was the largest ever to burn in the United States.

A roaring furnace

On August 19, as many as 3,000 fires were burning across Idaho and Montana, many of them started by lightning strikes in forests that had dried out over months of **drought.** Then, on August 20, hurricane-force winds roared through the forests. In a few hours, the fires developed into fire storms. Trees exploded from the heat or were ripped out of the ground by the force of the wind and hurled like flying torches to start new fires. Fireballs—great balls of burning gases—rolled along the ridgetops at 70 miles (113 kilometers) per hour or leapt across **canyons** hundreds of feet wide. Whole mountainsides caught fire and the separate fires became one huge fire.

Smoke blackened the sky, bringing night in the middle of the day. The crews of ships on the Pacific Ocean, some 500 miles (800 kilometers) away, could not see the stars to navigate. With the wildfire burning out of control, every able-bodied man in the region was drafted to fight the fire. The 10,000 men who battled the flames included soldiers, loggers, miners, and even panhandlers.

The Big Burn left 86 people dead, 78 of whom died trying to fight the fire. A few people killed themselves in terror as the fire approached. Flames shot hundreds of feet into the air, and arcs of fire sprang between

The area burned by the Big Burn of 1910.

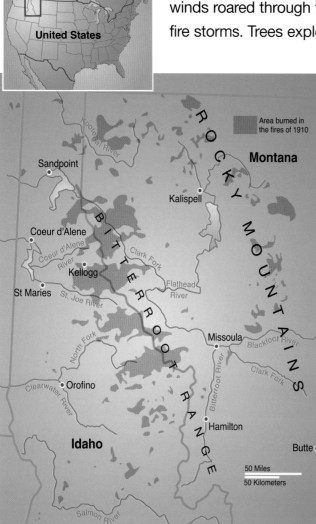

United States

Area burned in the fires of 1910

Sandpoint

Montana

Kalispell

Coeur d'Alene

ROCKY MOUNTAINS

Kellogg

Clark Fork

St Maries

Flathead River

St. Joe River

North Fork

Missoula

Blackfoot River

Clark Fork

BITTERROOT RANGE

Orofino

Clearwater River

Bitterroot River

Hamilton

Idaho

Butte

Salmon River

50 Miles

50 Kilometers

trees. One survivor described to a newspaper how "the fire turned trees and men into weird torches that exploded like Roman candles."

Ed Thenon was in charge of one of the crews battling the fire. He described the terrifying scene: "The wind had risen to hurricane velocity. Fire was now all around us, banners of incandescent flames licked at the sky. ... Men rushed back and forth trying to help. One giant, crazed with fear, broke and ran. I dashed after him. He came back, wild-eyed, crying, hysterical. The fire had closed in; the heat became intolerable."

LASTING EFFECTS

After a serious fire, the ground is left bare. Few roots remain to hold the soil in place, and a lack of plant cover exposes the land to wind and water. In some areas, **erosion** leads to flooding or **landslides** that can endanger settlements. Rain carries soil and **ash** into streams and rivers, killing fish. With no **vegetation** to provide food and shelter, wildlife must leave the area. At first, only a few types of plants regrow. Many years may pass before the previous variety of plants and animals returns. By the 2000's, most of the land scorched by the 1910 fire had returned to the state of a mature forest.

A plant ecologist in Yellowstone National Park measures the growth of lodgepole pine seedlings. Clearance of the ground by the 1988 fires (see page 15) allowed these seedlings to flourish.

On Oct. 19, 1991, firefighters **extinguished** a fire in Wildcat Canyon, near Oakland, California. The next day, the firefighters returned to check the area for any **hot spots** that were still smoldering. As the firefighters examined the **canyon,** gusts of wind restarted the fire. The blaze eventually blew into a **fire storm** that left 25 people dead and 150 others injured.

From conflagration to fire storm

The fire reignited near a developed area, and within 15 minutes it had reached its first building. Strong winds, sloping land, and plenty of fuel enabled the fire to spread quickly. After an hour, the firefighter in charge of the operation reported that it was "totally out of control and moving rapidly on several fronts, involving more than 100 acres (40 hectares) of trees, **brush,** and houses." About 790 homes burned down within that first hour.

From 20,000 to 30,000 people were evacuated before the fire reached Oakland. Most of the fire's victims died within the first half hour of its

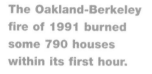

The Oakland-Berkeley fire of 1991 burned some 790 houses within its first hour.

FIRE-LOVING PLANTS

Many plants depend on fires to help them reproduce. Some of these plants grow in the **chaparral** areas around Berkeley and Oakland. Chaparral is a type of low, scrubby growth also found in the hot, dry European countries around the Mediterranean Sea. Such chaparral plants as chamise have root crowns from which new sprouts emerge after a fire. Others, including ceanothus and laurel, have seeds that start growing after exposure to the heat of a fire or to smoke. Aspen trees produce new growth from their roots after a fire. These plants regrow quickly in an area ravaged by fire.

Controlled fires in areas of scrub and chaparral in California are set regularly to prevent wildfires spreading into developed areas.

arrival. The majority of the deaths occurred as people tried to escape through narrow streets or became stuck in traffic jams, or because the victims were too old or disabled to escape. Many fire crews ran out of water to fight the blaze or were hampered by pipes that were too narrow to deliver water in sufficient quantity or force. In addition, fires caused power failures at pumping stations. At its peak, the fire burned 1 house every 11 seconds.

Under the right wind and temperature conditions, a fire becomes a **conflagration**—a raging, destructive fire. At some points, the Oakland-Berkeley fire was a conflagration, and at other times it was a fire storm.

Spotting and spreading

Like many fire storms, the Oakland-Berkeley fire produced long-distance **spotting,** which helped it to spread quickly. Some **embers** fell up to half a mile (0.8 kilometer) away, setting fire to the roofs of buildings and to dry vegetation. The wooden shingles used on houses in the area fed the fire. The city's narrow, winding roads prevented firefighters from moving around quickly to combat the spot fires. As the winds gradually died down, the firefighters were finally able to bring the blaze under control on October 25.

Wildfires have occurred throughout the history of Earth. Scientists have examined the charred remains of forest fires dating back 365 million years. This ancient evidence spans the world, from Antarctica—when its climate was moderate—to Norway. Clearly, before firefighters became involved, fires always burned themselves out.

No more fuel

A fire cannot continue to burn if it runs out of fuel. Fires die when they reach the edge of a body of water that they cannot cross, such as a wide river, a lake, or an ocean. A fire will also go out if it approaches an area with no **vegetation,** such as stony mountains, a desert, or an area that has already been burned. In a developed area, a wide highway can stop the advance of a fire. Firefighters often stop fires by creating **firebreaks,** which involves digging out vegetation or cutting down trees.

Firefighters dig a firebreak in Hells Canyon, Oregon, to slow or halt the spread of a fire.

The 1983 Ash Wednesday fires in Australia forced many people to evacuate their homes and move into temporary camps.

Changes in the landscape

Other aspects of **topography** can slow or stop a fire. At the crest of a hill, the upward incline that favors a fire changes to a downward slope that hinders its spread. As a fire goes downhill, its heat and **embers** escape upward without warming or torching vegetation ahead. Deep ravines and **canyons** can also stop a fire in its tracks.

Firefighters try to use natural barriers when fighting a wildfire. If the fire is contained on one side, firefighters will concentrate equipment and personnel in other areas where the fire can travel unhindered.

STOPPED BY THE SEA

The Ash Wednesday fires of Feb. 16, 1983, scorched much of Victoria in southeastern Australia. The fires burned over 1 million acres (400,000 hectares) and left 75 people dead. The ferocious blaze advanced rapidly in a four-day period. The fires stopped naturally when they burned to the edge of the ocean on Victoria's south coast.

INDONESIAN FIRES

In Indonesia, a severe fire season from 1997 to 1998 left nearly 24.7 million acres (10 million hectares) of forest in **ashes.** Some areas of the forest were a habitat for large numbers of endangered animals.

Naturally occurring fires have ignited frequently in Indonesia for thousands of years. But the number of fires each year has increased since the 1970's. Poor forest management is partly to blame for the change. People have removed established trees but have not replanted the forest. As a result, low-growing **brush** has grown to fill the gaps. Although the trees of the Indonesian rain forest have a natural resistance to fire, the brush burns easily and quickly, allowing fires to spread.

Deadly drought

The terrible fires of 1997 and 1998 resulted from conditions produced by an ocean and weather event called **El Niño,** which occurs about every two to seven years. During an El Niño, the weather in Southeast Asia becomes unusually dry. In Indonesia, **drought** and high temperatures commonly occur at these times, creating the ideal conditions for fire to take hold.

In 1997, the Indonesian government banned the use of outdoor fires because of the obvious dangers from the drought. But many farmers ignored the ban and continued to light fires to clear land. Some of these fires spread into the forests and raged over grass and scrubland.

An Indonesian boy plays in front of his house, where the land has been burned and cleared to make way for crops.

GLOBAL WARMING

Wildfires can contribute to **global warming** because they produce an enormous amount of carbon dioxide, one of the **greenhouse gases** that trap heat within Earth's atmosphere. Some scientists think that the Indonesian fires of 1997 and 1998 released as much carbon dioxide as all the vehicles and power stations in Europe do in a year. The carbon dioxide released into the atmosphere during the fires greatly contributed to the highest figure ever recorded.

Burning the ground

In many areas of Indonesia, the forest has been cleared because of **logging** and for palm oil cultivation. The removal of this protective layer of **vegetation** has caused the **peat** on the ground to dry out. Many fires that reached the edges of these dried peat bogs burned underground even after the visible fires in the forests had been put out or had run out of fuel. The dried peat continued to burn for months and burned down to a depth of between 10 and 33 inches (25 and 84 centimeters).

The smoke from the fires caused great human suffering. Hundreds of people died, and more than 40,000 people needed hospital treatment for conditions caused by breathing in smoke. The fires affected the health or livelihoods of 70 million people across much of Southeast Asia. In northern Sumatra, a plane crashed as a result of the smog, killing the 234 people on board.

Fires (highlighted in red in a satellite image) burn across parts of eastern Sumatra in March 2002. Strong winds drove the smoke across the island, creating a major air pollution problem. Some of Indonesia's frequent wildfires are actually set by farmers clearing land in the rain forest.

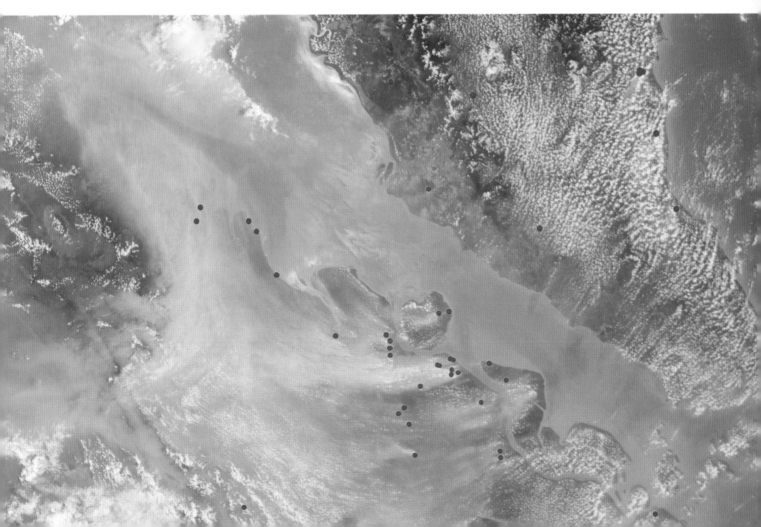

A fire lookout takes a bearing to locate the exact position of a fire in the Great Smoky Mountains National Park, Tennessee, in 1967.

A raging fire can quickly grow from a tiny spark. As a result, forest managers must monitor areas that commonly experience wildfires. Park authorities use well-organized systems to find and stop fires while they are still small.

Watching and waiting

Most fires occur during recognized fire seasons, when the land is dry and the weather is hot. Fire watchers monitor forests from lookout towers and spotter planes, searching for signs of smoke. In many areas, human fire watchers remain more effective and efficient than automated methods of tracking fire. Fire watchers also monitor the weather and forecasts for clues as to where fires might start. They may use satellite photographs for alerts about fires that are starting. Television cameras mounted around forests can provide extra information. Such measures work well in wealthy, developed countries. But some countries do not have enough money to build electronic fire-monitoring systems.

Fire towers

Indonesia, South Africa, and countries in Europe and North and South America use fire towers. Some fire towers are built of wood; others are made of metal. All fire towers consist of cabins built on top of a tall tower or on a natural area of high ground, such as tall rocks. Fire towers provide a wide view of the surrounding countryside. If a fire watcher in a tower sees smoke, he or she determines the approximate location of the fire and radios a local emergency center. The center responds by investigating and sending a fire crew if necessary.

HARNESSING TECHNOLOGY

Remote-sensing satellites and electronic **sensors** on the forest floor alert authorities to changes in temperature that signal the start of a fire. The sensors communicate with one another and directly with computers. Forest authorities use this equipment to carefully monitor some areas of forest that are not patrolled or watched from towers and planes.

Fire watchers monitor forests from lookout towers, such as the tower at Hat Point in Hells Canyon National Recreation Area, Oregon.

FIGHTING FIRES

Firefighters camp near Pine, Colorado, in June 2000 while battling a wildfire over the ridge behind the camp.

Firefighters must deliver an expert and prompt response to bring a wildfire under control. They use a variety of tools to investigate, attack, and clean up after fires.

Initial attack

When a fire is first spotted, fire authorities send an initial attack crew to investigate. The crew might include only a few firefighters. A **helitack crew** may arrive by helicopter. Or firefighters may drive in with a fire truck. Crews first slow the progress of a fire by dampening the area with water, foam or other **fire retardant.** Firefighters then try to contain the fire by clearing a **control line** around it, cutting down or burning forest and other **vegetation.** The control line has a band at the center, cleared down to bare dirt or rock, called the **fireline.** The crew uses such tools as axes, shovels, and bulldozers to remove all the fuel.

Fire camps

In the United States, if a fire grows to cover more than about 200 acres (80 hectares), firefighters set up a fire camp or incident base. At the fire camp, fire managers work out the best strategies to tackle the fire and make sure that firefighters and equipment go to the right locations.

Battling large fires

Firefighters cannot get close to large and intense fires. Instead, they create a control line some distance from the fire and let the fire burn within the line. As a last resort, firefighters may set a **backfire** within the control line. This is a dangerous procedure because fire crews must set the backfire in front of the approaching fire. Firefighters light a fire within the line so that it is drawn toward the main fire, burning out all the fuel. Fire crews plan backfires so that they burn a region twice as wide as the region over which the main fire burns. As a result, the main fire cannot jump over the backfire.

AFTER A FIRE

The fire crew finishes work by cleaning material from the edge of the burned area. They also cool any remaining **hot spots** to prevent other flare-ups. Firefighters can take days or even weeks to mop up after a large fire. The crews drench hot spots with water or foam. They also dig out underground hot spots to cool in the air. Firefighters do not cover hot spots with soil because it could lead to underground fires that reemerge later.

In a thermal image, active fires in California's San Bernardino Mountains are shown in yellow; previously burned but still hot areas appear dark red and purple. Taken from NASA's unmanned research aircraft Ikhana in October 2007, the image was superimposed onto Google Earth maps for use by firefighters.

GRASS VALLEY Lone Pine Island Lake Arrowhead Treasure Island

SLIDE

Fighting fires from above

Firefighters often find it impossible to reach a wildfire quickly over land. Sometimes, the fire itself poses a barrier to travel. In addition, fires often break out in areas with few or no roads or trails. In these cases, firefighters use planes and helicopters to attack fires from above. They drop water, foam, and fire-retardant chemicals onto the flames or onto areas just ahead of the fire. Helicopters use gigantic buckets to scoop up water from the sea, a lake, or a river and drop it on the fire. However, some fires have such intense flames, heat, wind, and smoke that aircraft cannot approach the blazes.

Ground-based firefighters work with watchers in planes who use infrared scanners, which detect different levels of heat intensity, to monitor different areas of the fire. These overhead scans provide a picture of how the fire is spreading.

A plane drops fire retardant on hot spots in California during a particularly devastating fire in 2003.

Smokejumpers

Smokejumpers are firefighters who parachute into a fire to fight it on the ground. Up to 18 smokejumpers may jump from a plane. Firefighting equipment is also dropped by parachute. After tackling the fire, the smokejumpers either walk from the scene or helicopters may pick them up.

Russia has about 2,000 smokejumpers, and there are nearly 300 in the United States. Smokejumpers must be very physically fit because they may have to carry more than 100 pounds (45 kilograms) of equipment and work very long hours. About half of all smokejumper recruits drop out during the first week of the four-week training program because of injury or lack of physical fitness.

THE MANN GULCH FIRE

On Aug. 5, 1949, 13 firefighters were killed by a fire in Mann Gulch in the Helena National Forest, Montana. The men belonged to a smokejumping team that had parachuted into the gulch to battle a small fire. But when the fire suddenly changed direction, the firefighters realized they were in danger. The foreman burned an escape fire to clear ground. He hoped his men could shelter there while the main fire passed. However, most of the firefighters tried to outrun the fire. Only three team members survived. Eventually, 450 firefighters brought the fire under control, but only after it had spread across about 4,400 acres (1,780 hectares) of forest. The loss of the firefighters had a great impact on firefighter training in the United States. Two years after the fire, the U.S. Forest Service opened two new smokejumper bases, one in Montana and one in Idaho. The service now has nine such bases, all located in the western United States. Researchers at the bases have developed fire-resistant clothing and fire shelters and have pioneered survival training programs.

SAVING PEOPLE AND BUILDINGS

The primary aim of a firefighter is to save people from fires. After people have been evacuated, a firefighter will try to save property. However, the firefighter's own safety must come first. Firefighters use a range of protective clothes and equipment that enable them to withstand the temperatures, smoke, and gases to which they are exposed. If firefighters cannot protect themselves, they cannot hope to save other people or property or stop the spread of a fire.

Safety for firefighters

Firefighters wear clothes made of special flame-resistant fabric. It can resist temperatures up to 1,200 °F (650 °C). If the fabric does burn, it chars rather than catches fire. Firefighters' protective boots and hard hats also provide protection. Firefighters are killed primarily by flames and smoke. Other causes of death include falling debris and vehicle accidents.

Firefighters carry a fire shelter for protection during emergencies. If they are overtaken by fire, they can lie inside this protective cocoon until the fire passes. The shelter consists of aluminum foil glued to fiberglass cloth. To use the shelter, the firefighter finds or clears a patch of ground, unfolds the cloth, and lies facedown inside the shelter. The shelter

A firefighter from the U.S. elite firefighting crew known as the "hotshots" uses a variety of ground and air techniques to manage wildfires.

THE THUMB FIRE

On Sept. 5, 1881, a terrible fire raged through the forest in Michigan's Thumb (east central) region. The blaze soon claimed human lives and buildings. The Thumb fire killed 282 people and left 15,000 others homeless. It started during a time of **drought,** when hurricane-force winds whipped hundreds of small land-clearing fires into a massive **conflagration.** By the time the fire burned itself out, 2.5 million acres (1 million hectares) had burned. The Thumb fire prompted one of the first major disaster relief efforts organized by the American Red Cross.

provides a pocket of breathable air. In addition, the aluminum reflects radiated heat, but the shelter can still become very hot inside.

A plane releases fire-retardant chemicals over houses that lie in the path of a wildfire. Smoke from the fire is visible on the far horizon.

Protecting people

Firefighters best protect people from fires by evacuating them to a safe area. Education about safe behavior during fires ranks as another important method of protection. But firefighters often have to rescue people from settlements overtaken by fire or people stranded in a forest. They may bring people out by truck, helicopter, or plane.

Saving buildings

After saving people, firefighters work to save buildings. People feel devastated when they lose their homes and communities to fire. Fire damage is often extremely costly. Fire crews try to protect buildings by creating **firebreaks** around settlements. In smaller fires, firefighters may cover buildings with **fire-retardant** chemicals and foams or drench them with water. When this approach succeeds, the fire causes little damage to buildings even if it burns the surrounding area.

WHAT TO DO IN A WILDFIRE

A firefighter demonstrates to a young boy how to handle a fire hose. The boy is taking part in a fire safety program about wildfires and controlled fires.

Many areas of the United States are prone to wildfires. Everyone living in these areas or visiting them must understand how to respond in the event of a fire.

Avoid danger

- If you are going into the forest or wilderness, use recognized roads and routes and plan your trip in advance. Leave a copy of your route so that you can be found and helped out of the area if necessary.
- If you see a wildfire, contact emergency services immediately. Go to a road or town.
- Fire travels most quickly with the wind and uphill. Go in the opposite direction—against the wind and downhill.

Only you can prevent forest fires

U.S. Department of Agriculture—Forest Service

In an emergency

- If you are stuck in the path of a fire, you will not be able to outrun it. Submerge yourself in a river or in the mud of a creek.
- Hot air poses the most danger. Try to lie down in a clear area of rock or sand if you can't find any water. Because hot air rises, lying down will put your face in the coolest area.
- As long as you have some other clothes, remove synthetic garments that might melt and stick to you.
- Remain calm. If you have to move to a safe spot, walk instead of running. Breathing in hot air poses the most dangerous risk. The worst of the fire will pass over you in 30 to 60 seconds.

A poster featuring Smokey Bear reminds people that it is up to each individual to play his or her part in preventing wildfires.

After the fire

- Take great care when walking through the burned area after a fire. Burning debris could fall on you, and the ground will be covered in scorching **embers.**
- If you have escaped from a wildfire, tell the authorities. Otherwise, people may risk their lives looking for you.

SAFE UNDERGROUND

People sometimes protect themselves from fire by burrowing into the ground. Many animals survive even fierce blazes by taking refuge underground. Demonstrate that soil can serve as an effective **insulator.**

Equipment

- A bucket
- A bag of soil
- A piece of string
- Two identical high temperature cooking thermometers
- A ruler
- A hair dryer

1. Put a thin layer of soil in the bucket. Tie the string around one thermometer and lay the thermometer horizontally on the soil. Drape the string over the side of the bucket so that it hangs down the outside.

2. Stand the ruler upright in the bucket. Put a little more soil in the bucket so that the bulb of the thermometer is covered but you can still see the scale. After two minutes, read the temperature off the thermometer and write it down.

3. Add more soil over the thermometer to a depth of 4 inches (10 centimeters).

4. Lay the other thermometer on top of the soil, directly above the first. Wait two minutes and write down the temperature of the top thermometer.

5. Use the hair dryer to heat the soil and the top thermometer for two minutes.

6. Turn off the hair dryer and immediately write down the temperature of the top thermometer.

7. As quickly as you can, pull up the bottom thermometer and note its temperature.

8. Compare the first and second temperatures you have recorded for each thermometer. How much did the temperature rise at the surface? How much did it rise below the soil?

aerial fuel Dead, dry vegetation more than 6 feet (1.8 meters) above the ground, including the leaves and branches of taller trees, which could fuel a fire.

arson The crime of deliberately and maliciously starting a fire.

ash A dry, powdery residue left after something has burned.

backfire A fire lit in the path of a wildfire to clear the area of fuel in an attempt to stop the fire.

brush A dense growth of bushes and shrubs.

bush Remote countryside of Australia.

canyon A rift in the land with high, steep sides.

chaparral A hot, dry area with dense, low-growing vegetation.

charcoal A brittle, black form of carbon left after a fire.

combustible Capable of burning.

combustion The action of burning.

conflagration A large and destructive fire.

conifer Any one of a group of trees and shrubs that produces cones containing its seeds.

control line A strip of land cleared of vegetation that is intended to set a limit to the area in which a fire can burn.

convection The movement of heat by currents of hot gas or liquid.

convection column A column of rising hot air or other gas.

convection current The movement in a liquid or gas caused by the tendency of hot masses to rise and cold masses to fall.

crown fire A fire that moves through the tops, or crowns, of trees.

drought A long period of unusually dry weather.

El Niño A warming of the surface water of the sea off the western coast of South America and a related weather change that happens every two to seven years.

ember A burning particle thrown out by a fire or left burning by a fire that has passed.

erosion Wearing away by the movement of water or wind.

eruption The pouring out of gases, ash, lava, and rocks from a volcano.

extinguish To put out a fire.

firebreak Land cleared of fuel to stop or slow the progress of a fire.

fireline A strip of land in the center of a control line that is scraped down to bare, mineral earth.

fire retardant A material that has significant resistance to damage or burning from fire.

fire storm An intense fire that fans its own flames by creating drafts.

fire whirl A tornadolike swirl of burning winds and flames.

flammable Easily set on fire.

global warming The gradual warming of Earth's atmosphere over many years.

greenhouse gas A gas that traps heat in Earth's atmosphere, contributing to global warming.

ground fire A fire that burns underground.

ground fuel Fuels that lie under the surface of the ground.

head (of a fire) The part of a fire that is advancing most quickly.

helitack crew A crew of firefighters that arrives by helicopter or uses a helicopter to fight fires.

hot spot (related to fires) An area that is hotter than the surrounding land.

insulator A material that prevents the passage of heat, electric current, or sound.

landslide A mass of soil and rock that slides down a slope.

logging Cutting down trees for timber.

meteorite A mass of stone or metal that reaches Earth from outer space without burning up in the atmosphere.

oxygen A gas present in the air that keeps a fire burning.

peat A layer of dead vegetation that has not decayed because of lack of oxygen.

ranger A person who looks after forests and their visitors.

sensor Any one of various devices that detect changes in temperature, radiation, motion, the depth of water, or the like.

spontaneous combustion The act of a material bursting into flames by being heated to a sufficiently high temperature, without being set alight by a spark or flame.

spotting The act of sparks or embers from a wildfire starting another fire ahead of the main fire.

surface fire A fire that burns surface fuels—the grass, leaves, and low shrubs on the ground.

surface fuel Fuel that lies on the ground, including grass, leaves, and low shrubs.

topography The form and surface features of the land.

updraft An upward movement of air.

vegetation Plants of all types.

volcano An opening in the crust through which ash, gases, and molten rock (lava) from deep underground erupt onto Earth's surface.

vortex A spinning column of wind and gas.

BOOKS

Blazing Bush and Forest Fires, by Louise and Richard Spilsbury, Heinemann Library, 2003.

Forest Furnace Wildfires, by Mary Colson, Raintree, 2004.

Under a Flaming Sky: The Great Hinckley Firestorm of 1894, by Daniel Brown, Lyons Press, 2006.

Wildfire, by Taylor Morrison, Houghton Mifflin, 2006.

Wildfire Alert! by Lynn Peppas, Crabtree Publishing, 2004.

Wildfires, by Paul P. and Diane M. Sipiera, Children's Press, 1998.

WEB SITES

http://oncampus.richmond.edu/academics/education/projects/webquests/disaster/scientist.htm

http://www.australiasevereweather.com/fires/index.html

http://www.idahoforests.org/fires2.htm

http://www.pbs.org/wgbh/nova/fire/simulation.html

http://www.smokeybear.com

INDEX